Kid's Trip Diary

Kid's Trip Diary

**Kids! Write about your own
adventures and experiences.
Have fun for hours!**

LORIS & MARLIN BREE
Authors of the best-selling
Kid's Travel Fun Book

MARLOR PRESS
ST. PAUL, MINNESOTA

Kid's Trip Diary

Revised edition

Special thanks to all the kids, educators, parents and others
who contributed to this book, especially Bernice Gutzmer.

ISBN 13: 978-1-892147-14-1
ISBN 10: 1-892147-14-9

Illustrations by Marlin Bree
Cover design by Theresa Gedig
Printed in the U.S.A.

MARLOR PRESS, INC.
4304 Brigadoon Drive
Saint Paul, MN 55126

CONTENTS

HOW TO HAVE FUN WITH THIS BOOK

Congratulations! You're going on a trip

SAY CHEESE!

PLEASE!

This book can help make your vacation a lot more fun. You can write about your own travel adventures and discoveries and play a new game every day. This book can be your friend for many happy travel hours.

Your **Kid's Trip Diary** is divided into three parts:

1/ Getting ready
2/ On the Road
3/ Memories

1/ Getting ready helps you get ready for your trip. You can make plans for what you want to see and do. It's fun to think about your vacation.

2/ On the Road is for when you travel. You write about your adventures. You tell what you did, what you liked best, and what you saw. There are ideas every day for a new game for you to play. Wow, some vacation!

3/ Memories. All good vacations come to an end, but you will have a souvenir after your trip is over. Paste in a ticket to a fun park, a picture you took or a postcard. Save your best memories of your trip and your people.

A SPECIAL NOTE TO PARENTS

This book will make traveling more fun for your child. It will also make it easier for him or her to travel with the family.

When a child takes part in preparing for a vacation or a trip, he or she makes an investment in the journey. A child can look forward to travel as fun and adventure.

Help your child get information about where you are going. You can do this on the Internet or you can get a book or a magazine. It will be exciting to see photos and information.

Help your child make a short list of what he or she wants to see and do on the trip. This lets your child anticipate the trip as a fun adventure.

Help your child prepare for the trip. Children should help decide what to take along on the trip. They can help pack their own bags of clothing and supplies. You can also help the child fill out information to take along, such as **Who I want to send messages to.** You can make this a positive experience by your attitude and your words. Travel is fun if there's lots to do.

Keep in mind that children will be discouraged by criticism or even the suggestion that what they've done could be improved. If your child is too small to write, just ask the child to tell you what he or she wants to say. Remember to write the short, simple sentences your child uses. You don't have to be fancy but your child will remember your love and your interest.

Children enjoy having a little money of their own. On the **Daily Diary** pages, they can record what they spend and their daily totals. This teaches money management and can help make the vacation special.

It's important to be very supportive of children during travel. Give them your attention and encouragement. Tell them when you think what they have done is wonderful. Always be positive and soon you will see gradual improvement in their communication abilities. Relax and let your child have fun with this book. You will both have a better time on vacation.

A checklist of fun things to take

▶A game bag filled with different play things. Your child can open a new one each day

▶Washable markers and colored pencils to draw in the **Kid's Trip Diary**

▶Maps of the trip with your route marked. Your child can also mark places where you stop

▶Spending money for your child to carry and use. (Be sure to have your child mark this down in the **Daily Diary's** *What I bought today)*

▶Small pillow to make your child comfortable

▶Healthy snacks and healthy drinks to avoid sugar. (Keep these in a cooler if you are traveling by automobile or van)

▶A portable cassette or CD player, along with the child's favorite music or spoken books. (Perhaps purchase a new one—or get one from the library?)

▶Magazines and books. Bring some old favorites plus some new ones from the library. Bring a copy of **Marlor's Kid's Travel Fun Book.**

▶Some extra writing supplies, such as a large paper tablet

▶A small cardboard box for special travel souvenirs, such as picture postcards, small souvenirs or tickets to parks or rides

▶Several favorite books for reading aloud

PART ONE

GETTING READY

- What I want to do before I go
- What I want to see and do on my trip
- What I want to take along
- Important information to take with me
- Who I want to send messages to
- I don't want to forget

FIVE
STEPS
TO GET
READY

Adventure ahead! There are lots of things to think about and to learn.

1/ What I want to do before I go: Think about what you need to do before you go. Do you have a pet that needs someone to take care of it? A plant that needs watering? Books to return to the library? Write these things down on **Page 11.**

2/ What I want to see and do on my trip: Travel is fun. Find out about your trip and where you are going. Talk about some things you'd like to do. You can visit the Internet. You can read books or magazines at the library and you can write for information to the state or city you plan to visit. From the things you find out, write down what you would like to see and do on **Page 12.**

3/ What I want to take along: Think about the games, toys and clothes you want to take with you. Remember it is easier to pack things, especially toys, that are small. Write on **Page 13.**

4/ Important to take along: Write down the information you want to keep with you. These can be friends and family names as well as emergency telephone numbers. Write on **Page 14.**

5/ Who I want to send messages to: Think of how pleased a special friend, grandparent or an aunt will be when they get a note or a postcard from you. Write down the names and addresses of these people on **Page 15.**

1

WHAT I WANT TO DO BEFORE I GO

VACATIONS ARE AWESOME!

1/ XASe the bathroom

2/ _____

3/ _____

4/ _____

5/ _____

6/ _____

7/ _____

8/ _____

9/ _____

10/ _____

11/ _____

12/ _____

2

WHAT I WANT TO SEE AND DO ON MY TRIP

1/ _____

2/ _____

3/ _____

4/ _____

5/ _____

6/ _____

7/ _____

8/ _____

9/ _____

10/ _____

11/ _____

12/ _____

3

WHAT I WANT TO TAKE ALONG

EVERYTHING

1/ _____

2/ _____

3/_____

4/ _____

5/ _____

6/ _____

7/ _____

8/ _____

9/ _____

10/ _____

11/ _____

12/ _____

wow!

4

IMPORTANT
INFORMATION
TO TAKE
WITH ME

MY NAME _____

My home address _____

My city _____ State _____ Zip _____

My home telephone (Area Code   ) _____

Height _____ Weight _____ Age _____

The adult I am with _____

Where we will stay _____

_____

In an emergency, please contact at home

Name _____

Telephone (Area Code _____) _____

My Doctor or Clinic _____

Telephone (Area Code   ) _____

My special medical needs: _____

5

WHO
I WANT
TO SEND
MESSAGES TO

Name _____

Street Address _____

City _____ State _____ Zip _____

E-mail _____

Name _____

Street Address _____

City _____ State _____ Zip _____

E-mail _____

Name _____

Street Address _____

City _____ State _____ Zip _____

E-mail _____

Name _____

Street Address _____

City _____ State _____ Zip _____

E-mail _____

5.

I DON'T
WANT
TO
FORGET!

Perhaps you will want to remind yourself to pack a **special game** or a **special toy.** Or to send **notes** home to friends. List these things below.

1/ —————————————————————————

2/ —————————————————————————

3/ —————————————————————————

4/ —————————————————————————

5/ —————————————————————————

6/ —————————————————————————

7/ —————————————————————————

8/ —————————————————————————

9/ —————————————————————————

10/ ————————————————————————

PART TWO

ON
THE
ROAD

- How to use your *Daily Diary*
- Your *Daily Diary Pages*
- Extra games to play
- Extra puzzles

EASY!

HOW TO USE YOUR DAILY DIARY

Some easy-to-use
tips and examples

Y ou can jot something down for every day of your
trip. It's fun and it helps you keep a wonderful
record.

■ You can tell about each day of your trip in **Today's Diary.**

■ You can have **two pages** for every day of your trip. There are enough pages for 28 days. If you go on a shorter trip, you can use more pages when you write. You can use more pages if you have a lot to tell.

■ On the following pages, you can see examples from the **Today's Diary** pages. You can see suggestions for writing for each of the pages.

■ There's also a place each day for you to draw something!

■ There is a **new game** for each day of your trip

■ You'll find some **extra games** in the back of the book.

1. At the top of the left page you begin with **Today's Date**, what **Our weather Is**, and **Today We Are In.** You don't have to be fancy about describing the weather or where you are. You can just say something like "sunny" or " it rained all day." Talk to your adults about where you are for the **Today We Are In.** Look at the example below. Easy, isn't it?

TODAY'S

TODAY'S DATE: **MONDAY, JULY 7**

OUR WEATHER IS: **SUNNY!**

TODAY WE ARE IN: **ORLANDO, FLORIDA**

2. Next, you can tell something about what you did today in **What We Did today.** Just a few words will do. Then be certain you write down **Things I Liked Best.** See the example below.

WOW!

WHAT WE DID TODAY: **We spent the day at Disneyland. What fun!**

THINGS I LIKED BEST: **The Pirate ride!**

3. Perhaps **something funny** happened to you or someone with you. Or you saw something you felt good about. Write it down.

HOW ABOUT SOME TREASURE?

WHAT I SAW OR HEARD THAT WAS FUNNY: **The Pirates**

4. Here you can list some of the **favorite things** you ate or drank today. Be certain to tell if you really liked them.

SOME FOODS I ATE: **Hot dogs.**
Really pigged out

5. You may have a little **travel money** to spend and to record. Write down what you bought today and how much you spent.

ITEM	WHAT I BOUGHT TODAY	COST
	Pirate Hat	$ 10.95
	Pirate "T" Shirt	12.00
	TOTAL THAT I SPENT TODAY	$ 22.95

6. At the end of the day, you can **add up** what you spend. Then you can figure out how much money you have left. Do you have to make your money last for the entire trip? Maybe you will want to put it in a pile for each day left. Then you'll know how much you have left to spend.

7. Draw a picture of something you liked today.
Have fun with your drawing.

8.You can write a few words explaining a little about
your picture. It will be fun to look back at what you drew
and said at the end of the trip.

MY PICTURE IS ABOUT **Mister "M"**
Mouse and me!

9. If you write just a little bit, and
draw a picture a day, you will have
a fine time keeping a diary of your
trip. You will have many good memories when your trip is over.

TODAY'S

TODAY'S DATE: _____

OUR WEATHER IS: _____

TODAY WE ARE IN: _____

_____

WHAT WE DID TODAY: _____

_____

_____

THINGS I LIKED BEST: _____

_____

WHAT I SAW OR HEARD THAT WAS FUNNY:

_____

_____

SOME FOODS I ATE: _____

_____

ITEM	**WHAT I BOUGHT TODAY**	COST
_____		$ _____
_____		_____
_____		_____
_____		_____
	TOTAL THAT I SPENT TODAY	$ _____

DIARY

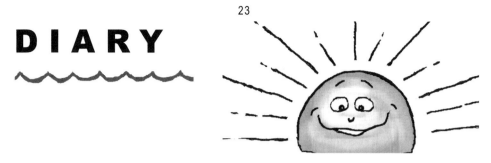

DRAW SOMETHING YOU SAW TODAY

MY PICTURE IS ABOUT _____

SIGNS OF THE TIMES

**NO RAIN
ALLOWED
TODAY!**

Don't we wish we could put up a sign that says, "no rain allowed today?" that way we could always have sunshine on our trip. But there are real signs you see as you travel. Today's game is for you to try to make **words** from signs, beginning with **alphabetical** letters in order. The first person to see an **A** on a sign calls out **"A."** The next person to see a B calls out that letter. Get the idea? Letters must be in order. The person who sees the most letters from A to Z wins. Fun, huh?

TODAY'S

TODAY'S DATE: _____

OUR WEATHER IS: _____

TODAY WE ARE IN: _____

_____

WHAT WE DID TODAY: _____

_____

_____

THINGS I LIKED BEST: _____

_____

WHAT I SAW OR HEARD THAT WAS FUNNY:

_____

SOME FOODS I ATE: _____

_____

ITEM	**WHAT I BOUGHT TODAY**	COST
_____		$_____
_____		_____
_____		_____
_____		_____
	TOTAL THAT I SPENT TODAY	$ _____

DIARY

DRAW SOMETHING YOU SAW TODAY

MY PICTURE IS ABOUT_____

THE TOWER OF DOOM

The **Tower Doom** lies somewhere ahead. You will get caught in the Tower if you say the **Forbidden Word,** which you agree on in advance. It can be any ordinary word; in fact, the more ordinary the better.That's so you can trip up your players and send them to the **Tower of Doom**, where they have to remain silent for the next 5 miles or 5 minutes. Good words *not* to be spoken are *yes, no*, or the toughest of all, *I*. You can talk about anything, but the person who says the **Forbidden Word** is banished. To vary the game after a while, you can have several **Forbidden Words.**

TODAY'S

TODAY'S DATE: ————————

OUR WEATHER IS:————————

TODAY WE ARE IN: ————————

————————————————

WHAT WE DID TODAY: ————————————————

————————————————————————

THINGS I LIKED BEST: ————————————————

GOOD ONE, MATEY!

————————————————————————

WHAT I SAW OR HEARD THAT WAS FUNNY:

————————————————————————

SOME FOODS I ATE: ————————————

————————————————————————

ITEM	**WHAT I BOUGHT TODAY**	COST
————————————————————		$ ————
————————————————————		————
————————————————————		————
————————————————————		————

TOTAL THAT I SPENT TODAY $

DIARY

AVAST, MATIES!

DRAW SOMETHING YOU SAW TODAY

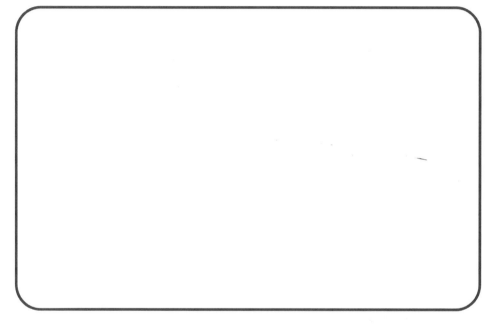

MY PICTURE IS ABOUT _____

TRUE COLORS

Pick a **favorite color** and look for objects that are this color. For example, as you drive down the highway, you can say, "I see a red barn." Or, "I see a red car." The object is to see who can get the most objects of the chosen color in 5 minutes. Each player in turn can choose a different color. After you play this game for a while, you can make it a little harder by saying what you will or will not count. For example, you could count only objects of a chosen color, which are not cars. Or trucks or SUV's.

HAVE A BALL?

TODAY'S

TODAY'S DATE: _____

OUR WEATHER IS: _____

TODAY WE ARE IN: _____

_____

WHAT WE DID TODAY: _____

_____

THINGS I LIKED BEST: _____

_____

LOVE HAVING A BALL!

WHAT I SAW OR HEARD THAT WAS FUNNY:

_____

SOME FOODS I ATE: _____

_____

ITEM	**WHAT I BOUGHT TODAY**	COST
		$
_____		_____
_____		_____
_____		_____
_____		_____
TOTAL THAT I SPENT TODAY		$

DIARY

DRAW SOMETHING
YOU SAW TODAY

HOOP LA!

MY PICTURE IS ABOUT _____

YOU SEE W-H-A-T?

I SEE

The first player **looks about**, perhaps out of the window of the car, then gives **one clue** such as *"I see something red."* The others have to guess what he or she sees. Each player has one guess. The winner gets to be in charge of the next round of **I See.**

TODAY'S

~~~~~~~~~~

TODAY'S DATE:_____

OUR WEATHER IS:_____

TODAY WE ARE IN: _____

_____

WHAT WE DID TODAY: _____

_____

_____

THINGS I LIKED BEST:_____

_____

WHAT I SAW OR HEARD THAT WAS FUNNY:

_____

SOME FOODS I ATE: _____

_____

WHAT I BOUGHT TODAY   COST

_____ $ _____

_____   _____

_____   _____

_____   _____

TOTAL THAT I SPENT TODAY $

DIARY

DRAW SOMETHING YOU SAW TODAY

MY PICTURE IS ABOUT _____

I PACKED MY BAG

You've probably never packed a bag like this before where you are limited only by your imagination. Name an **object to pack** and then say, *"I packed my bag,"* and add: *"in it I have a car"* or whatever you decide.) Then the next player says, *"I packed my bag and in it I have a car and a bar,"* (or whatever the player decides to add). By the time the game gets going, you'll all have quite a bag. The objective of the game is to **name everything in the bag in sequence,** or the player is out. The winner is the last player who names everything correctly.

TODAY'S

TODAY'S DATE: _____

OUR WEATHER IS: _____

TODAY WE ARE IN: _____

_____

WHAT WE DID TODAY: _____

_____

THINGS I LIKED BEST: _____

_____

YOU SAY SOMETHING?

WHAT I SAW OR HEARD THAT WAS FUNNY:

_____

SOME FOODS I ATE: _____

_____

ITEM	**WHAT I BOUGHT TODAY**	COST
_____		$ _____
_____		_____
_____		_____
_____		_____
	TOTAL THAT I SPENT TODAY	$

DIARY

**DRAW SOMETHING
YOU SAW TODAY**

MY PICTURE IS ABOUT _____

_____

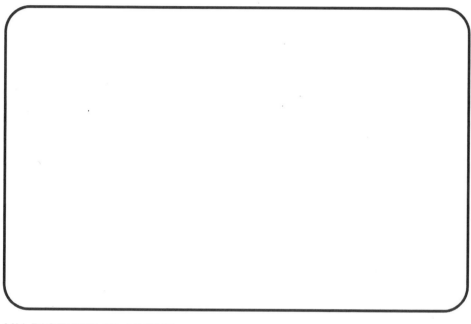

SCRAMBLE UP

Take a blank piece of paper and on it **scramble a word s**o that it is not rec-
ognizable. For example, you can scramble the word, *travel,* by changing the
letters around it to make it read, *"velart,"* which is travel scrambled up. The
game is for the rest of the players to figure out what the scrambled word is
and put the letters in correct order on their piece of paper to identify the word.
It's only fun that the best unscrambler gets to be the next word scrambler.

TODAY'S

THUMB'S UP!

TODAY'S DATE: _____

OUR WEATHER IS: _____

TODAY WE ARE IN: _____

_____

WHAT WE DID TODAY: _____

_____

_____

THINGS I LIKED BEST: _____

_____

LIKED BEST?

UMM

WHAT I SAW OR HEARD THAT WAS FUNNY:

_____

SOME FOODS I ATE: _____

_____

_____

ITEM | **WHAT I BOUGHT TODAY** | COST

_____ $_____

_____ _____

_____ _____

_____ _____

TOTAL THAT I SPENT TODAY $ _____

DIARY

WAY UP

DRAW SOMETHING YOU SAW TODAY

MY PICTURE IS ABOUT _____

PURR-FECT

THE STATE GAME

The leader names a **state** and the players figure out what the **last letter** is of that state and then name another state that begins with the **last letter.** For example, if the leader calls *Minnesota,* then the last letter is an *A*. So the game is to think of states that begin with *A*. (Hint: Alaska or Alabama, to name just two). The winner gets to name **another state** and the game begins all over again. A variation is to play with the names of well-known countries (France, Japan, etc.) or world famous cities (Paris, London), instead of state names.

TODAY'S

YEAH! IT'S RAINING

TODAY'S DATE: _____

OUR WEATHER IS: _____

TODAY WE ARE IN: _____

_____

WHAT WE DID TODAY: _____

_____

_____

FUN!

THINGS I LIKED BEST: _____

_____

MORE RAIN!

WHAT I SAW OR HEARD THAT WAS FUNNY:

_____

SOME FOODS I ATE: _____

_____

ITEM   **WHAT I BOUGHT TODAY**   COST

_____ $ _____

_____   _____

_____   _____

_____   _____

TOTAL THAT I SPENT TODAY $

DIARY

A LITTLE RAIN TODAY?

DRAW SOMETHING
YOU SAW TODAY

MY PICTURE IS ABOUT _____

ENOUGH RAIN!

NAME THAT TUNE!

Now you get a chance to be a little **musical** (or a lot). One player names a **category** such as rain songs (*Singing in the Rain*, for example) or a **word**. The other players in turn get to name that tune. Some suggestions: songs that are about dances, favorite films or TV shows, travel, people's names, seasons, times of the day (such as sunset or night), or about romance. For a variation, the winner (or the loser) gets to sing them. Or, everybody sings them!

TODAY'S

HOO-RAH BEARS!

TODAY'S DATE:_____

OUR WEATHER IS:_____

TODAY WE ARE IN: _____

_____

WHAT WE DID TODAY: _____

_____

_____

THINGS I LIKED BEST: _____

_____

BEARS ARE THE GREATEST

WHAT I SAW OR HEARD THAT WAS FUNNY:

_____

SOME FOODS I ATE: _____

_____

ITEM	TOTAL THAT I SPENT TODAY	COST
_____		$ _____
_____		_____
_____		_____
_____		_____
	TOTAL THAT I SPENT TODAY	$ _____

DIARY

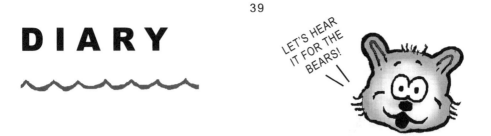

LET'S HEAR IT FOR THE BEARS!

DRAW SOMETHING YOU SAW TODAY

MY PICTURE IS ABOUT_____

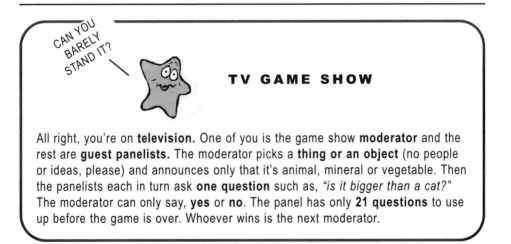

CAN YOU BARELY STAND IT?

TV GAME SHOW

All right, you're on **television.** One of you is the game show **moderator** and the rest are **guest panelists.** The moderator picks a **thing or an object** (no people or ideas, please) and announces only that it's animal, mineral or vegetable. Then the panelists each in turn ask **one question** such as, *"is it bigger than a cat?"* The moderator can only say, **yes** or **no**. The panel has only **21 questions** to use up before the game is over. Whoever wins is the next moderator.

TODAY'S

LOVE IT!

TODAY'S DATE: _____

OUR WEATHER IS: _____

TODAY WE ARE IN: _____

_____

WHAT WE DID TODAY: _____

NEED RAIN

_____

THINGS I LIKED BEST: _____

_____

MORE SUN!

WHAT I SAW OR HEARD THAT WAS FUNNY:

_____

SOME FOODS I ATE: _____

_____

ITEM	**WHAT I BOUGHT TODAY**	COST
_____		$ _____
_____		_____
_____		_____
_____		_____
	TOTAL THAT I SPENT TODAY	$ _____

DIARY

DRAW SOMETHING
YOU SAW TODAY

MY PICTURE IS ABOUT _____

TALE TELLERS

Everyone loves a good story, especially if you don't know where it will end. In **Tale Tellers,** someone **starts a story** that he or she makes up. At an exciting place, the moderator calls *Stop*. Then the next person continues telling the story **his or her way** with some **variations.** Sometimes the story really gets switched around. At another exciting place, another *Stop* is called and another tale teller takes over. Sometimes the next tale teller will go on with the story by saying, *"But while this was happening.."* You get the idea. The story goes on for as long as tale tellers tell tales. And you know how long that *can be.*

TODAY'S

FOLD A MAP? **ME?**

TODAY'S DATE: _____

OUR WEATHER IS: _____

TODAY WE ARE IN: _____

_____

WHAT WE DID TODAY: _____

_____

THINGS I LIKED BEST: _____

_____

AARGH!

EASY!

WHAT I SAW OR HEARD THAT WAS FUNNY:

_____

SOME FOODS I ATE:

_____

_____

ITEM	**WHAT I BOUGHT TODAY**	COST
_____		$ _____
_____		_____
_____		_____
_____		_____
	TOTAL THAT I SPENT TODAY	$ _____

DIARY

DRAW SOMETHING YOU SAW TODAY

MY PICTURE IS ABOUT _____

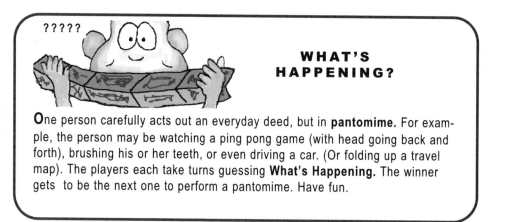

WHAT'S HAPPENING?

One person carefully acts out an everyday deed, but in **pantomime.** For example, the person may be watching a ping pong game (with head going back and forth), brushing his or her teeth, or even driving a car. (Or folding up a travel map). The players each take turns guessing **What's Happening.** The winner gets to be the next one to perform a pantomime. Have fun.

TODAY'S

IT'S SUNNY, OF COURSE

TODAY'S DATE: _____

OUR WEATHER IS: _____

TODAY WE ARE IN: _____

_____

WHAT WE DID TODAY: _____

_____

_____

SUNNY ALL DAY?

THINGS I LIKED BEST: _____

_____

MY BEST VACATION!

WHAT I SAW OR HEARD THAT WAS FUNNY: _____

_____

SOME FOODS I ATE: _____

_____

ITEM	**WHAT I BOUGHT TODAY**	COST
_____		$ _____
_____		_____
_____		_____
_____		_____
TOTAL THAT I SPENT TODAY		$ _____

DIARY

DRAW SOMETHING YOU SAW TODAY

MY PICTURE IS ABOUT _____

HOTTER OR COLDER?

The main player decides on an **object** within the car or room and then everyone in turn tries to learn what that is. The main player will say *hotter* when the guesses are in the right direction and *colder* when the guesses are going the wrong way. The winner gets to be the main player and select a new object to find.

TODAY'S

IT'S WIZARDLY!

TODAY'S DATE:_____

OUR WEATHER IS: _____

TODAY WE ARE IN: _____

_____

WHAT WE DID TODAY:_____

_____

_____

FUN!

THINGS I LIKED BEST: _____

_____

BUNNIES LIKE MAGIC TOO

WHAT I SAW OR HEARD THAT WAS FUNNY:

_____

SOME FOODS I ATE: _____

_____

ITEM	**WHAT I BOUGHT TODAY**	COST
		$ _____
_____		_____
_____		_____
_____		_____
_____		
	TOTAL THAT I SPENT TODAY	$ _____

DIARY

IT'S MAGIC

DRAW SOMETHING YOU SAW TODAY

MY PICTURE IS ABOUT _____

LIKE THAT?

MAGIC MIRROR

One person is chosen to be the **mirror** and the rest of the players *mirror him or her* for two minutes. The game is that each player must be an **exact mirror image** of the mirror, often with funny results (some people are cracked mirrors). Here are some basic things the group might try to mirror: stick out a tongue, laugh heartily, cross eyes, wink one eye at a time, meow piteously, pretend to drive an SUV, fly an airplane or sail a boat in a storm. Wow.

FWIP

WANT TO STOP FOR A BITE?

FWIP FWIP

TODAY'S

TODAY'S DATE: _____

OUR WEATHER IS:_____

TODAY WE ARE IN: _____

_____

WHAT WE DID TODAY: _____

_____

BOOM!

THINGS I LIKED BEST: _____

NOTHING EVER HAPPENS ON VACATION!

_____

WHAT I SAW OR HEARD THAT WAS FUNNY:

_____

SOME FOODS I ATE:_____

_____

_____

ITEM	**WHAT I BOUGHT TODAY**	COST
		$
_____		_____
_____		_____
_____		_____
_____		_____
	TOTAL THAT I SPENT TODAY	$ _____

DIARY

DRAW SOMETHING
YOU SAW TODAY

MY PICTURE IS ABOUT _____

EEK! HOW AWFUL

Into a **paper bag,** secretly collect a few ordinary items such as a grape, a sock, a feather, a paper clip, a coin, and so forth. Use your imagination. Players in turn close their eyes, then insert their fingers to feel and touch the object and to describe it. *Eek How Awful.* You'll be surprised how imaginative the answers can get from touching and feeling everyday things.

TODAY'S

BURP! BURP!
SORRY

TODAY'S DATE: _____

OUR WEATHER IS: _____

TODAY WE ARE IN: _____

_____

WHAT WE DID TODAY: _____

B-R-A-P!

_____

_____

THINGS I LIKED BEST: _____

_____

GOOD TO
WARM UP
FIRST

WHAT I SAW OR HEARD THAT WAS
FUNNY: _____

_____

SOME FOODS I ATE: _____

_____

ITEM   **WHAT I BOUGHT TODAY**   COST

$

_____   _____

_____   _____

_____   _____

_____   _____

TOTAL THAT I SPENT TODAY

$ _____

DIARY

BURP!
EXCUSE
ME

DRAW SOMETHING
YOU SAW TODAY

MY PICTURE IS ABOUT _____

BURP

FOLLOW ME

Everyone follows the **leader's activity** and then adds **one activity.** For example, the leader can start the game by holding his or her nose. The next person has to follow this example and then add one more activity, such as sneezing. The next person in turn holds his or her nose, sneezes and then adds something new, like snapping fingers. The game goes on with each player repeating the previous activity and then repeating what went on before. The player who misses a thing is out. The winner is the one who repeats everything.

TODAY'S

FAIR WINDS TODAY

TODAY'S DATE: _____

OUR WEATHER IS: _____

TODAY WE ARE IN: _____

_____

WHAT WE DID TODAY: _____

_____

_____

WHAT'S THAT AHEAD?

THINGS I LIKED BEST: _____

_____

TREASURE!

WHAT I SAW OR HEARD THAT WAS FUNNY:

_____

_____

SOME FOODS I ATE:

_____

_____

ITEM	**WHAT I BOUGHT TODAY**	COST
		$
_____		_____
_____		_____
_____		_____
_____		_____
TOTAL THAT I SPENT TODAY		$ _____

DIARY

DRAW SOMETHING
YOU SAW TODAY

LOOK
ALIVE,
MATIES

MY PICTURE IS ABOUT _____

CHARADES

A PIE RAT?

The leader will make up a **charade** and the rest will try to guess. The subject can be the name of a **TV show, a movie, book** or a **song title.** The leader will hold up **fingers** to indicate **number** of words. Then the leader will hold up a finger to indicate the first word, second word, and so on, while performing a charade. Everyone tries to guess what's going on. The winner is the player who guesses the full name or title. Then that person is the leader.

LOOK HERE!

TODAY'S

TODAY'S DATE: _____

OUR WEATHER IS: _____

TODAY WE ARE IN: _____

_____

WHAT WE DID TODAY: _____

_____

_____

I GOT LOTS!

THINGS I LIKED BEST: _____

_____

HAVE ONE!

WHAT I SAW OR HEARD THAT WAS FUNNY:

_____

SOME FOODS I ATE: _____

_____

ITEM   **WHAT I BOUGHT TODAY**   COST

$

_____   _____

_____   _____

_____   _____

_____   _____

TOTAL THAT I SPENT TODAY $ _____

DIARY

DRAW SOMETHING
YOU SAW TODAY

HEY! WANT A BANANA?

MY PICTURE IS ABOUT _____

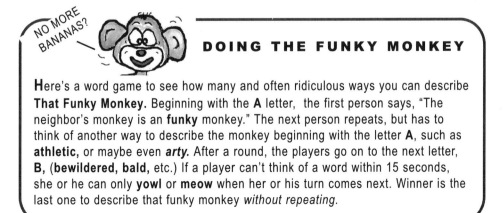

NO MORE BANANAS?

DOING THE FUNKY MONKEY

Here's a word game to see how many and often ridiculous ways you can describe **That Funky Monkey.** Beginning with the **A** letter, the first person says, "The neighbor's monkey is an **funky** monkey." The next person repeats, but has to think of another way to describe the monkey beginning with the letter **A**, such as **athletic,** or maybe even *arty.* After a round, the players go on to the next letter, **B,** (**bewildered, bald,** etc.) If a player can't think of a word within 15 seconds, she or he can only **yowl** or **meow** when her or his turn comes next. Winner is the last one to describe that funky monkey *without repeating.*

TODAY'S

FUR ME?

TODAY'S DATE: _____

OUR WEATHER IS: _____

TODAY WE ARE IN: _____

_____

WHAT WE DID TODAY: _____ BUNNIES ARE GOOD

_____

THINGS I LIKED BEST: _____

_____

JUST ASK ONE

WHAT I SAW OR HEARD THAT WAS FUNNY:

_____

SOME FOODS I ATE: _____

_____

ITEM	**WHAT I BOUGHT TODAY**	COST
_____		$ _____
_____		_____
_____		_____
_____		_____
TOTAL THAT I SPENT TODAY		$ _____

DIARY

DRAW SOMETHING
YOU SAW TODAY

MY PICTURE IS ABOUT _____

BUNNIES
SAY THINGS,
TOO!

SIMON SAYS

One player is Simon and only Simon gives the orders. The object is to *only* follow the orders specifically preceded by the words, **"Simon Says."** For example, if Simon says *"sit up"* and a person sits up, then that person is out of the game. However, if Simon says *"Simon says sit up,"* that's a correct order. Once Simon starts giving orders quickly, one by one the players will drop out. Some examples of orders: *"Hold out your hands...hands up.* **Simon says,** *hands up. Turn around...look right."* Of course, Simon has to say it first for it to be a proper command. The winner gets to be Simon.

TODAY'S

TODAY'S DATE: _____

OUR WEATHER IS: _____

TODAY WE ARE IN: _____

_____

WHAT WE DID TODAY: _____

_____

_____

THINGS I LIKED BEST: _____

_____

DANCE

DANCE

WHAT I SAW OR HEARD THAT WAS FUNNY:

_____

SOME FOODS I ATE: _____

_____

DANCE

BIG FINISH!

ITEM	**WHAT I BOUGHT TODAY**	COST
		$ _____
_____		_____
_____		_____
_____		_____
TOTAL THAT I SPENT TODAY		$

DIARY

SOMETIMES YOU JUST FEEL LIKE DANCING

DRAW SOMETHING
YOU SAW TODAY

MY PICTURE IS ABOUT _____

HO, HO, HO!

In this game, the first player says **"ho."** The second player adds, **"ho, ho!"** And so on around the ring of players, each adding a ho-hoing in his or her own way. Each must *"ho"* in the right number and each add a new *"ho"*. With a little imagination, the ho-hoing can be hilarious. Anyone can laugh, except the person ho-hoing. That person must not laugh while ho-hoing or else be eliminated from the game. The one who has the most staying power and remembers the right number of ho-hoes is the winner.,

OH, OH!

TODAY'S

TODAY'S DATE: _____

OUR WEATHER IS: _____

TODAY WE ARE IN: _____

_____

WHAT WE DID TODAY: _____   EVERYBODY'S
                                         DOING IT

_____

_____

THINGS I LIKED BEST: _____

_____

HI, MASKED
FRIENDS

WHAT I SAW OR HEARD THAT WAS FUNNY:

_____

SOME FOODS I ATE: _____

_____

_____

ITEM	**WHAT I BOUGHT TODAY**	COST
_____		$ _____
_____		_____
_____		_____
_____		_____
	TOTAL THAT I SPENT TODAY	$ _____

DIARY

DRAW SOMETHING
YOU SAW TODAY

MY PICTURE IS ABOUT _____

DUPLICATING MACHINES

One person begins the game by making some **motion**, such as rubbing his or her nose. Then that person points to another player, who in turn, has to **duplicate** what the first player has done and **add one more motion**. This player points to another player who has to duplicate all that has gone on before and, you guessed it, add one more motion. All motions have to be in proper sequence. The winner is the one who duplicates all motions and in sequence.

SOMEBODY SAY FOOD?

TODAY'S

TODAY'S DATE: _____

OUR WEATHER IS: _____

TODAY WE ARE IN: _____

_____

WHAT WE DID TODAY: _____

_____

_____

THINGS I LIKED BEST: _____

_____

WHAT I SAW OR HEARD THAT WAS FUNNY:

_____

SOME FOODS I ATE: _____

_____

ITEM	**WHAT I BOUGHT TODAY**	COST
		$
_____		_____
_____		_____
_____		_____
_____		_____
TOTAL THAT I SPENT TODAY		$ _____

DIARY

DRAW SOMETHING YOU SAW TODAY

MY PICTURE IS ABOUT _____

OPPOSITES

They say that **opposites attract** and in fact, one opposite will attract another in this game. Choose up sides so each person has an "opponent." In turn each opponent says **one word** and his or her opponent says the **opposite** of the word. For example, one says *no,* the other *yes; stormy, fair skies, hot, cold, spicy, bland,* and so on. Each player has only three seconds to answer. The player giving the correct answers without making a mistake wins.

WHEN IS THE NEXT REST STOP?

TODAY'S

TODAY'S DATE: _____

OUR WEATHER IS: _____

TODAY WE ARE IN: _____

_____

WHAT WE DID TODAY: _____

THAT FAR?

_____

_____

THINGS I LIKED BEST: _____

_____

NO MORE SUPER-SIZE DRINKS!

WHAT I SAW OR HEARD THAT WAS FUNNY: _____

_____

SOME FOODS I ATE: _____

_____

ITEM **WHAT I BOUGHT TODAY** COST

_____ $ _____

_____ _____

_____ _____

_____ _____

TOTAL THAT I SPENT TODAY $ _____

DIARY

OH, NO!

DRAW SOMETHING YOU SAW TODAY

MY PICTURE IS ABOUT _____

WHAT RHYMES WITH SOON?

RAPPING WITH RHYMES

Here's your chance to do some **"raps" with words** you see along the way, such as on billboards or signs. For example, if you see a sign that says *Stop Ahead,* you can use it in a rhyming rap that goes, *"If you don't / Stop ahead / You won't / Get fed."* Or, *"Supersized drinks / Lots of fun / Except when you need a rest stop / And there is none."* Everybody takes turns or players can be chosen to rap with signs that everyone sees. (*And if you don't/ See any signs/ You're just not going to have/ A real good time.*)

TENNIS, ANYONE?

TODAY'S

TODAY'S DATE:_____

OUR WEATHER IS:_____

TODAY WE ARE IN: _____

_____

WHAT WE DID TODAY:_____

_____

_____

THINGS I LIKED BEST: _____

_____

BAM!

GOOD SERVE!

WHAT I SAW OR HEARD THAT WAS FUNNY:

_____

SOME FOODS I ATE: _____

_____

ITEM **WHAT I BOUGHT TODAY** COST

_____ $ _____

_____ _____

_____ _____

_____ _____

TOTAL THAT I SPENT TODAY $ _____

DIARY

DRAW SOMETHING
YOU SAW TODAY

MY PICTURE IS ABOUT _____

MINDREADER

The moderator announces he or she has a **famous person** in mind. This person may be living or dead but must be famous enough for everyone to recognize. The moderator says only the **first initial** of the **last name.** The mindreaders have to guess the **name** of the famous person by asking questions beginning with, *"Are you concentrating on___?"* The questions can only be by category, such as, *"Are you concentrating on a famous actress?"* Or, ..."a rock star?" or, *"an historical figure?" "Still alive?" "A woman?"* and so on until the famous person whose name begins with the letter is **"guessed."**

TODAY'S

WHY? WHY?

TODAY'S DATE:_____

OUR WEATHER IS:_____

TODAY WE ARE IN:_____

_____

WHAT WE DID TODAY: _____

_____

_____

THINGS I LIKED BEST:_____

_____

SO UNFAIR

WHY CAN'T I DO IT AGAIN?

WHAT I SAW OR HEARD THAT WAS FUNNY:

_____

SOME FOODS I ATE: _____

_____

ITEM **WHAT I BOUGHT TODAY** COST

_____ $ _____

_____ _____

_____ _____

_____ _____

TOTAL THAT I SPENT TODAY $ _____

DIARY

DRAW SOMETHING
YOU SAW TODAY

MY PICTURE IS ABOUT _____

CRAZY PICTURES

Take a sheet of paper and **fold it in thirds.** On the **top third**, unknown to the others, the first player draws the **head and neck** of a person, animal or thing. The page is then folded over so that just the bottom of the picture shows. The next player draws the **body** on the second third of the page. Of course, the second player should not know what the first player was drawing. The third player gets to finish the bottom third of the sheet by drawing the **legs and the feet.** Unfold the sheet and there you have a **crazy picture.** Perhaps you can even think of a fun name for your creation. *Crazy, huh?*

TODAY'S

YOO HOO

ME

MY DATE TODAY: _____

MY WEATHER IS: _____

TODAY I AM IN: _____

_____

WHAT I DID TODAY: _____

_____

_____

WHAT I LIKED BEST: _____

_____

THIS ONE'S FOR ME

FEELS GOOD!

WHAT I THOUGHT WAS FUNNY: _____

_____

SOME FOODS I ATE: _____

_____

_____

ME

ITEM	**WHAT I BOUGHT TODAY**	COST
_____		$ _____
_____		_____
_____		_____
_____		_____
	TOTAL THAT I SPENT TODAY	$ _____

DIARY

WHEE! ALL FOR ME!

MY DRAWING OF SOMETHING I SAW TODAY

MY PICTURE IS ABOUT _____

FAMOUS ME!
(It's about time)

Here's a chance to be a **star** or a **celebrity**. One person is **Famous Me**, a person well known in history, television, motion pictures, books or sports. The players in turn ask the "celebrity" questions to find out his or her identity. The famous person can only answer with a *yes* or a *no*. (Or a nod or shake of the head). The limit is 16 questions. Whoever guesses right can be the next famous person.

NOT ME

TODAY'S

TODAY'S DATE: _____

OUR WEATHER IS: _____

TODAY WE ARE IN: _____

_____

WHAT WE DID TODAY: _____

_____

_____

THINGS I LIKED BEST: _____

_____

ULP!

EVER HAVE ONE OF THOSE
DAYS WHEN YOU THINK
PEOPLE ARE STARING AT YOU?

WHAT I SAW OR HEARD THAT WAS FUNNY:

_____

SOME FOODS I ATE: _____

_____

ITEM   **WHAT I BOUGHT TODAY**   COST

_____ $ _____

_____   _____

_____   _____

_____   _____

TOTAL THAT I SPENT TODAY $

DIARY

**DRAW SOMETHING
YOU SAW TODAY**

OH, NO!

MY PICTURE IS ABOUT _____

POPEYE

This is a game you can play at night. Look for a car with just **one headlight.**
The first person to see this yells, **"Popeye,"** and gets to touch, slap or light-
ly punch the person next to him or her on the shoulder. *Agree* on what you
are going to do in *advance*, and be careful: don't hit too hard, please!

TODAY'S

TODAY'S DATE: _____

OUR WEATHER IS: _____

TODAY WE ARE IN: _____

_____

WHAT DO YOU SAY?

WHAT WE DID TODAY: _____

_____

_____

THINGS I LIKED BEST: _____

_____

MAY I HAVE SOME MORE?

WHAT I SAW OR HEARD THAT WAS FUNNY:

_____

SOME FOODS I ATE: _____

_____

ITEM   **WHAT I BOUGHT TODAY**   COST

$ _____

_____   _____

_____   _____

_____   _____

_____   _____

TOTAL THAT I SPENT TODAY $ _____

DIARY

BURP!

DRAW SOMETHING
YOU SAW TODAY

MY PICTURE IS ABOUT —————————————————————

I SPY

All the players become **spies** on the lookout for something they agree upon in advance. This can be most anything. For example, if the players are in a moving car or van, that can be a red barn. Everyone tries to locate a red barn. The first one to see one cries, *"I spy."* He or she gets one point. If two say *I spy* at the same time, each get one point. Whoever gets to 10 points first wins and gets to pick the next object. Objects can be a bridge, a red car, a yellow sign, a horse, or even a car with a certain license plate, such as a Minnesota plate.

TODAY'S

FUN! FUN!

TODAY'S DATE: _____

OUR WEATHER IS: _____

TODAY WE ARE IN: _____

_____

WHAT WE DID TODAY: _____

_____

_____

THINK FUN!

THINGS I LIKED BEST: _____

_____

TRY HAVING FUN

WHAT I SAW OR HEARD THAT WAS FUNNY:

_____

SOME FOODS I ATE: _____

_____

ITEM	**WHAT I BOUGHT TODAY**	COST
_____		$ _____
_____		_____
_____		_____
_____		_____
	TOTAL THAT I SPENT TODAY	$ _____

DIARY

DRAW SOMETHING YOU SAW TODAY

MY PICTURE IS ABOUT _____

CONTACT

While you're traveling in the family vehicle, try this game of coordination. Choose an object **you can see** not too far ahead, such as a historical marker, a landmark, or even a fast-food restaurant. All players (except the driver, of course) close their eyes and when each thinks the chosen object is exactly alongside, the player hollers *"contact,"* opens her or his eyes. Winner is the person who guesses correctly or is closest. An alterative to this group game is for each player in turn to play **contact.**

COMING ALONG?

EXTRA GAMES TO PLAY

Going on a sailing trip?

You're going sailing for a long time and you have to take some things along with you. Trouble is, you can only take along things beginning with the letter **S** (for sailboat). So can your crew. You begin by saying, *"I'm going on a sailing trip and I'm taking along a snake."* Your other players also have to repeat what you said and then add one more thing of their own. This must also begin with an **S**. Those who forget the sequence or who can't think of anything beginning with an **S** are out. The winner is the last person still going. You can start the game all over again with a new letter.

Tic Tac Toe
TWO WAYS

TWO WAYS, MATEY!

WAY ONE: On a piece of paper, draw two lines up and two lines sideways to form a grid (see below). Each player in turn gets to place a mark of an X or an O in each small square. Rows must be vertical, diagonal or horizontal. The player that gets three marks in a row wins. The looser starts the next game.

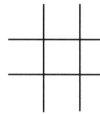

SAMPLE GRID   DOTTED LINES ABOVE INDICATE WINNING PLAYS

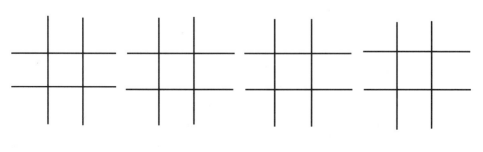

SCORE: ME _____ MY OPPONENT_____

WAY TWO: You can play a variation on **Tic Tac Toe** by making the grid with the same four lines, but then **closing the ends** into a **box**. Instead of playing the boxes, you play your **X** and O's where the **lines meet** (on the intersections). Take a look at the examples below. Get the idea? You need three letters in a row to win.

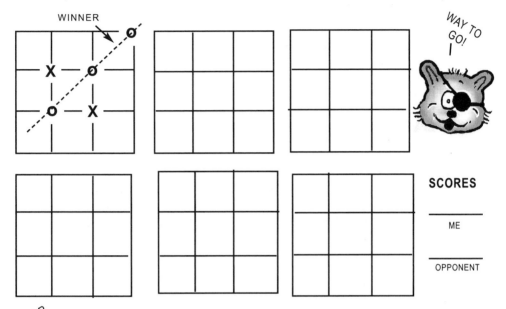

WINNER

WAY TO GO!

SCORES

_____
ME

_____
OPPONENT

B IS FOR BEAR

ALPHABET GAME

As you travel, look for signs that have **letters.** Begin looking for the letter **A.** Write that below and the initials of the person who first saw it. Then look for the letter **B** and so on. You need to go in alphabetical order. The first person to name the letter gets the point. The player with the most points wins.

A _____
B _____
C _____
D _____
E _____
F _____
G _____
H _____
I _____
J _____
K _____
L _____
M _____

N _____
O _____
P _____
Q _____
R _____
S _____
T _____
U _____
V _____
W _____
X _____
Y _____
Z _____

THE COLOR PURPLE

The main player picks something inside the car, train or plane (however you're traveling) which is a certain **color**, such as *purple.* He or she then says, "*Color me **purple**.*" The players try to guess what object he or she has chosen. If a couple of rounds don't locate the specific item, then players can ask specific questions on its **size or location**. The winner gets to pick the next color and object. A variation: You can say **hotter** when the guessing gets close to the object; **colder** when it's not.

BLIND ARTIST

Get a sheet of paper and a pencil. **Blindfold** whoever is **It** and then place the tip of the pencil on the paper. The blindfolded person is then told **what to draw,** such as an airplane, a car or a ship. The fun comes when everyone sees what the blind artist tries to draw. Take turns.

CROSS THE CREEK

Here's a game for inside your motel room. Get some pieces of **paper** (maybe a paper towel) and lay pieces in an **irregular line**, but stepping distance apart. These are **stepping stones**. Each person has to step carefully or else he or she will end up in the creek. The rules are that only one foot can be on a "stone" at a time. For an added variation after a couple of games, certain really smart persons can also **balance a book** on their heads. If they step off the "stone" or lose their book, they fall in the creek and are out.

FWIP!

IT'S A GOAL!

In your room, a **wastebasket** can become a **basketball hoop.** Sheets of paper are wadded up into **"balls,"** or socks are rolled together into balls. Each player gets a toss. As everyone gets better at the game, the basket can be moved farther away. First one to get to **21 points** wins. After a while, you can also place the goal against a wall for bank shots, or prop it at an angle against a chair. Have a ball.

T W O

PENNY GAMES

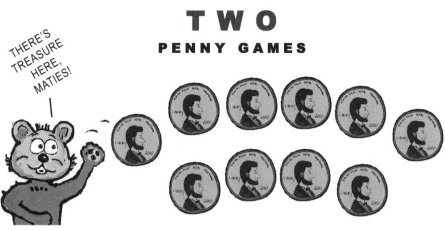

LUCKY PENNIES

You will need **10 pennies*** per player. Taking turns, each player secretly puts a number of pennies in his or her **closed hand.** The object of the game is to take turns guessing how many pennies the player has in hand. *Winner gets the pennies.* But if the guessers do not name the correct amount in the hand, they **lose** from their hoard the amount the player had in hand. For example, if the player had 3 pennies in hand, then each guesser would lose 3 pennies for the wrong guess. **Hint:** play with just a few pennies at first.

ODD OR EVEN?

A longer-lasting variation: You can play this game with just one opponent. The player again secretly places from **one to ten pennies** in his or her **closed hand** and then places the hand in front of the opponent. The opponent must guess **odd** or **even** amounts of pennies. If he or she is right, the opponent *wins a penny.* If he or she is incorrect, the opponent *loses a penny.* The game goes on until no pennies are left to play with or after a certain amount of time has gone by, the winner is declared as the one with the most pennies.

*Note: You can also play this game with toothpicks, marbles, or other small objects.

WHAT ARE THESE
PICTURES
TRYING TO TELL US?

(The answer is at the bottom of the page.)

CHARADE
PICTURES

You play this game by **drawing pictures**, instead of **acting out** a **charade.** The first player chooses a topic, as in charades. She or he can choose from a title of a popular kid's book, a well-known song, or a hit movie. Also, the player can choose a funny or contemporary saying, or the title or something from a famous nursery rhyme. The fun part is that the player can't use any words.

On a piece of paper, he or she **draws** pictures representing the charade. The opposing players try to guess the subject. The person who guesses the topic the quickest is the winner and gets one point. Then it's time to change players and the winner has a turn to be the main player.

You can also divide into teams if you like and decide jointly how you want to present your subject. Have fun!

ANSWER: The picture at the left shows a cow making a *mooing* noise. In the center picture, a boy is jumping up (see his feet?) In the last picture, we see a moon. What is the Picture Charade? If you guessed, *The Cow Jumped Over the Moon,* you were 100 percent correct.

GUESS THE
PICTURE
CHARADES

Here are some **charade pictures** for you to guess (or to use in your games.) The answers are at the bottom of the page. No peeking!

1

2

ROCK!

3

OINK   OINK   OINK

4

HEAR   TED

5

+UP

6

+ OFF

FENCING KIDS

It's sort of like a mini **fencing match** in which you and your opponent can make thrusts with you trusty pencil. You can fence **sideways** and **up and down** *between the dots*. You **can't** move *diagonally*. Each player gets **one move** at a time to connect **two dots.** Then it's the other player's turn. Your goal is to complete a square to put your **initial** in it. Then you get another turn. If you see someone else closing a square you can block their move by putting in your line when your turn comes. And of course you have to be careful not to get caught connecting the third side of a box when your turn comes, because then your opponent can close the box to claim the point. The champion kid fencer is the one with the most squares. **Game hint:** different colored pencils help keep track of each player. Or one player can use a line and another a series of dots.

ROUND 1

ROUND 2

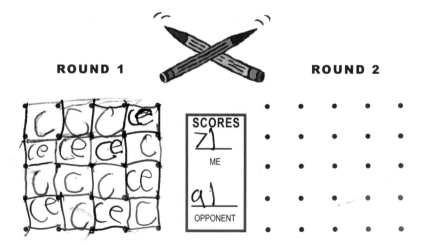

SCORES

71

ME

91

OPPONENT

ROUND 3

ROUND 4

ROUND 5

SCORES

_____
ME
_____
OPPONENT

ROUND 6

ROUND 7

ROUND 8

ROUND 9

ROUND 10

ROUND 11

SCORES

ME

OPPONENT

ROUND 12

ROUND 13

ROUND 14

ROUND 15

ROUND 16

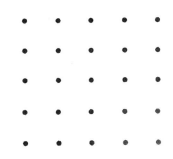

ROUND 17

SCORES
ME
OPPONENT

ROUND 18

ROUND 19

ROUND 20

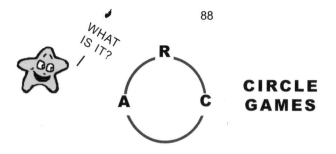

CIRCLE GAMES

Try to find the **words** spelled out below. Each circle contains just **one** word. Your job is to figure out the word. You must find the **starting letter** and then read **clockwise** (the way a clock turns). You can't skip a letter. For example, in the circle game above, the starting letter is **C**. Reading clockwise, you'll find that the word is **CAR.** (Don't peek, but the answers are on the bottom of the page, upside down).

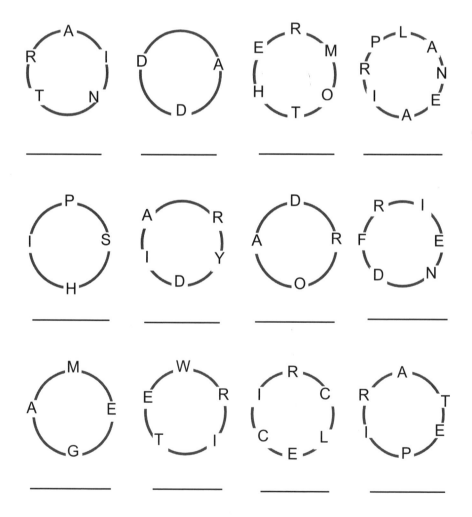

WORD GAMES

Rapid Riddles

1/ What do you have that others use more than you when you travel?

2/ What smells the most in the car?

3/ It falls down all the time but never gets hurt. What is it?

4/ You give this away all the time but still you can keep it. What is it?

5/ What kind of coat can you put on wet and still be happy with?

6/ What is black and white but red all over?

7/ What's very light but you can't hold for very long?

8/ What is faster: hot or cold?

9/ What word do you always pronounce wrong?

10/ Even when the world seems dark and gloomy, where can you always find happiness?

Silly States: Are you in Enw Orky?

Oh, my! Someone has misspelled the following **states** and you have to be a detective and put them back in order. For example, **Sotaminne** isn't a new soft drink. It's the state of **Minnesota**, all scrambled up. Here are some more states for you to unscramble.

1/ Sinconwis
2/ Sexta
3/ Enw Orky
4/ Ouths Kotada
5/ Nooger

6/ Ippssimissm
7/ Drifalo
8/ Sillioni
9/ Enaim
10/ Doahi

RAPID RIDDLES ANSWERS: 1/ Your word 2/ Your nose 3/ Rain 4/ Your word 5/ Coat of paint 6/ A newspaper (red is read) 7/ Your breath 8/ Hot, because you can catch cold 9/The word, wrong 10/ In your dictionary

SILLY STATES ANSWERS: 1/ Wisconsin 2/ Texas 3/ New York 4/ South Dakota 5/ Oregon/ 6/ Mississippi 7/ Florida 8/ Illinois 9/ Mine 10/ Idaho

CAR GAMES

Try to identify each of the following. Write your initials if you are the first to see each item. The winner is the one who has seen the most subjects the first.

— Car with open trunk

— Car with hood up

— Car with trailer hitch

— Car with door open

— Car the same kind and color as your own

— Car with spare tire carried on rear end

— Car with hood up

— Convertible car (with or without top down)

— Station wagon

— Volkswagen "beetle"

— Car with luggage on top

COLORFULLY YOURS

Try to find things that are of the following **colors**. The first to see these colors writes it down and puts his or her name after each.

White _____

Black _____

Blue _____

Red _____

Green _____

Orange _____

Pink _____

Yellow _____

PART
THREE

MEMORIES

■ Memories:Things I saved from my trip

■ Names, addresses & places to remember

■ My final thoughts about this trip

WONDERFUL
IDEA!

SCRAP
BOOK
MEMORIES

Here you can keep small, personal **mementoes** of your vacation. Some **souvenirs** you might want to keep are **ticket stubs** to a favorite place or a fun ride, a picture **postcard** you picked out, or **small printed materials** you saved from places you visited.

A few favorite things
I saved from my trip

More ideas: If you went abroad, save some foreign **currency** samples. You can add a favorite **photograph** or two. Under each item, be sure to write a **few words** that will help you remember, such as the date, where you were, & what it was like *Be creative.*

MORE

MEMORIES

FROM MY TRIP

NAMES, ADDRESSES & PLACES TO REMEMBER

Travel is an adventure. You will be making new friends as you travel as well as seeing interesting places. Here you can write down names & addresses so that later you can keep in touch.

1/ NAME _____

ADDRESS _____

CITY _____ STATE _____ ZIP _____

E-MAIL _____ TELEPHONE _____

COMMENTS _____

2/ NAME _____

ADDRESS _____

CITY _____ STATE _____ ZIP _____

E-MAIL _____ TELEPHONE _____

COMMENTS _____

3/ NAME _____

ADDRESS _____

CITY _____ STATE _____ ZIP _____

E-MAIL _____ TELEPHONE _____

COMMENTS _____

4/ NAME _____

ADDRESS _____

CITY _____ STATE _____ ZIP _____

E-MAIL _____ TELEPHONE _____

COMMENTS _____

MY FINAL WORDS
ON THIS TRIP

Did you have a good time? What did you especially like? Did you have some worst moments (Hint: Every trip has these). Would you change anything the next time? Lastly, you can rate your trip on a scale of 1 to 10. Make 10 the very best and 1 the worst ever. Be honest, now

MY FINAL COMMENTS _____

_____

_____

I ESPECIALLY REMEMBER THESE GOOD TIMES

_____

_____

_____

MY WORSE MOMENTS _____

_____

_____

WHAT I'D DO DIFFERENTLY THE NEXT TIME I TRAVEL

_____

_____

_____

**ON A SCALE OF 1 (WORST)
TO 10 (BEST)
I'D RATE THIS TRIP
A BIG FAT**

_____

MY RATING